DATE DUE

EXXON VALDEZ

HOW A MASSIVE OIL SPILL TRIGGERED AN ENVIRONMENTAL CATASTROPHE

by Michael Burgan

Content Adviser: Michael Wert, PhD
Associate Professor of History
Marquette University

COMPASS POINT BOOKS
a capstone imprint

Compass Point Books are published by Capstone,
1710 Roe Crest Drive, North Mankato, Minnesota 56003
www.mycapstone.com

Editor: Catherine Neitge
Designer: Catherine Neitge
Media Researcher: Svetlana Zhurkin
Library Consultant: Kathleen Baxter
Production Specialist: Laura Manthe

Image Credits
AP Photo: Al Grillo, 43, Bob Stapleton, 45; Bridgeman Images: State Central Navy
Museum, St. Petersburg/*Fur Traders of the Russian-American Company, 1989* (oil
on cardboard), Pshenichny, Igor Pavlovich (b. 1938), 15; DVIDS: U.S. Coast Guard
Photo, 7, 27, 58 (top), 59 (top); Getty Images: Al Grillo, 41, Bettmann, 11, 56
(bottom), Corbis/Natalie Fobes, 29, MCT/*Anchorage Daily News*/Bob Hallinen, cover,
39, *National Geographic*/Natalie B. Fobes, 9, 36, *National Geographic*/Steven L.
Raymer, 5, The *LIFE* Picture Collection/Nat Farbman, 19; The New York Public Library
Digital Collections, 17; Newscom: MCT/*Anchorage Daily News*/Bob Hallinen, 35,
55, 58 (bottom), MCT/*Anchorage Daily News*/Erik Hill, 32, 53, MCT/Chuck Kennedy,
50, Photoshot/Bruce Coleman/J.E. Swedberg, 31, TNS/Staff, 10, Zuma Press/Adn/
Loren Holmes, 23, Zuma Press/Arlis, 48, Zuma Press/Gary Braasch, 13, Zuma Press/
St. Petersburg Times/Will Vragovic, 28; Shutterstock: EQRoy, 57 (top), Everett
Historical, 56 (top), Gail Johnson, 21, Jon Nicholls Photography, 47, Joseph Sohm,
24, 57 (bottom), Wildnerdpix, 59 (bottom)

Library of Congress Cataloging-in-Publication Data

Names: Burgan, Michael, author.
Title: Exxon Valdez : how a massive oil spill triggered an environmental catastrophe
/ by Michael Burgan.
Description: North Mankato, Minnesota : Capstone Press, [2018] | Series: CPB grades
4-8. Captured science history | Audience: Age 10-14. | Includes bibliographical
references and index.
Identifiers: LCCN 2017037863 (print) | LCCN 2017041958 (ebook) | ISBN
9780756557515 (eBook PDF) | ISBN 9780756557430 (hardcover) | ISBN
9780756557478 (paperback)
Subjects: LCSH: Exxon Valdez Oil Spill, Alaska, 1989—Juvenile literature. |Oil spills—
Alaska—Prince William Sound Region—History—20th century—Juvenile literature. |
Oil spills—Environmental aspects—Alaska—Prince William Sound Region—History—
20th century—Juvenile literature. | Tankers—Accidents—Alaska—Prince William
Sound Region—History—20th century—Juvenile literature. | Exxon Valdez (Ship)—
Juvenile literature. | Environmental disasters—Juvenile literature.
Classification: LCC TD427.P4 (ebook) | LCC TD427.P4 B87 2018 (print) | DDC
363.738/2097983—dc23
LC record available at https://lccn.loc.gov/2017037863

Printed in Canada.
010798S18

TABLEOFCONTENTS

ChapterOne
THE BIG ONE COMES

In the small town of Valdez, Alaska, a group of about 30 residents crowded around a speakerphone in a local government office. It was Thursday evening, March 23, 1989, and the Easter weekend was about to begin. On the other end of the line was Riki Ott, an expert in marine science. Like many of the people in Valdez and other small towns along Alaska's Prince William Sound, she also fished. Salmon and herring filled the waters of the sound. Fishing was an important part of the local economy—the money fishers made selling their catch helped businesses stay open. The sound was also home to bald eagles and other birds that caught the fish for food, along with sea otters, sea lions, orcas, and other mammals. Many of these animals also relied on the fish to survive.

Another natural resource besides fish had become important to the local economy, and to Alaska as a whole. In June 1977 oil had begun flowing from Alaska's Prudhoe Bay, above the Arctic Circle, through the Trans-Alaska Pipeline System (TAPS). For 800 miles (1,287 kilometers), the pipeline crosses some of the coldest and most isolated parts of the United States. Finally the oil reaches the Valdez Marine Terminal. There it is loaded on giant ships called tankers, which take the oil to be turned into gasoline and other petroleum-based products.

Oil storage tanks lined the shore of the harbor in Valdez, Alaska, when oil began flowing through the Trans-Alaska Pipeline System in 1977.

Many fishers on Prince William Sound, along with some indigenous Alaska people, had opposed the building of the pipeline and the terminal. They feared an oil spill could ruin their way of life. For the native Alaskans, that included hunting sea mammals that lived in the sound as well as catching fish. But with backing from the U.S. government, several oil companies were able to drill for the oil buried beneath the frozen Arctic land and transport it to other states.

The fear of an oil spill and pollution from the Valdez Marine Terminal had not faded in the years after TAPS opened. Ships leaving the terminal sometimes had accidents, even though a major spill hadn't occurred. Riki Ott was one of the people worried about a spill. She could not attend the meeting in Valdez on March 23 because bad weather had made it impossible to fly there from her home in the small fishing town of Cordova on Prince William Sound. No roads linked the two communities, so flying would have been the fastest way there. Instead, Ott sat by herself in a room 70 miles (113 km) away and spoke to the people at the meeting in Valdez by phone.

Ott talked about the increasing number of tankers sailing to and from the Valdez terminal through the sound. Many of the ships, she noted, were getting too old to operate safely. And she warned that if a spill happened in open waters, it might not be contained and cleaned up quickly. Ott said "the big one"—a massive oil spill in Prince William Sound—was bound to happen. "It's not if, but when it occurs, and we're not going to be prepared as a community."

As Ott spoke on the phone, a ship loaded with oil was about to leave the Valdez Marine Terminal. The *Exxon Valdez* was almost 1,000 feet (305 meters) long, and, as its name suggested, it was owned by Exxon, one of seven companies that operated the pipeline and terminal. The seven had formed the Alyeska

When it was delivered in 1986, the *Exxon Valdez* was the largest ship ever built on the U.S. West Coast.

Pipeline Services Company in 1970. Exxon was the largest of the companies involved and the largest U.S. oil company.

That night at about 9:20, the *Exxon Valdez* slowly made its way out of the port carrying 53 million gallons (200 million liters) of fuel oil. Commanding the ship was Captain Joseph Hazelwood. At 42, he had worked for Exxon for 19 years, and he had won safety awards from the company in 1987 and 1988. But as the *Exxon Valdez* ship headed into the sound, Hazelwood was not on the bridge giving course and speed commands. As was usually done, a harbor pilot guided the tanker through a narrow waterway about 7 miles (11 km) out of the port. Hazelwood came to the bridge shortly after 11 p.m., before the pilot left the ship.

Hazelwood soon saw on radar that large chunks of ice had drifted into the path that he would normally take to reach the open sea. The ice had broken off the nearby Columbia Glacier. The captain contacted the U.S. Coast Guard's Vessel Tracking Center in Valdez to explain the situation. The center followed the movement of all ships coming into and leaving Valdez. The center gave Hazelwood permission to use the sea-lane that ships normally used to enter the harbor. After a while, Hazelwood left the bridge, leaving third mate Gregory Cousins in charge of putting the ship back on its usual course once it passed the ice.

But something went wrong as the huge ship cut through the waters of Prince William Sound. Lookout Maureen Jones entered the bridge and told Cousins the ship was mistakenly on the wrong side of a buoy light. Cousins ordered a shift in course to try to get on the right side of the buoy, but the tanker could not respond quickly enough. Just after midnight on March 24—Good Friday—Cousins called down to Hazelwood's cabin. "Sir," the third mate said, "I think we have a serious navigational problem." Still on the phone, Cousins felt a series of bumps, as the steel hull of the ship smashed into the rocks of Bligh Reef. The sailors quickly realized that their ship was aground. They and Hazelwood also soon discovered that the collision had ripped holes in the ship's hull. Millions of gallons of Prudhoe Bay oil were now flooding into Prince William Sound.

"Sir, I think we have a serious navigational problem."

Through holes in its smashed steel hull, the tanker *Exxon Valdez* spilled millions of gallons of oil into Prince William Sound.

At 12:26 a.m., Hazelwood radioed the Coast Guard to say the *Exxon Valdez* was aground. He added, "And, ah, evidently, [we're] leaking some oil and we're gonna be here for awhile." Hazelwood tried to rock the ship off the reef, though that had its own dangers. A computer report showed that the ship could sink without the rocks holding it up. Hazelwood finally gave up trying to free the ship, as more oil poured out of its holds.

News of the crash and oil spill spread to all the organizations responsible for preventing such a spill and cleaning one up if one did occur. Along with the Coast Guard, other U.S officials soon knew

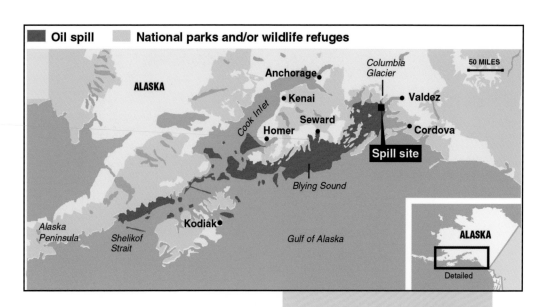

| Oil spill | National parks and/or wildlife refuges |

ALASKA

Anchorage
Kenai
Cook Inlet
Homer
Seward
Columbia Glacier
Valdez
Spill site
Cordova

Blying Sound

Alaska Peninsula
Shelikof Strait
Kodiak
Gulf of Alaska

50 MILES

ALASKA
Detailed

about the situation at Bligh Reef. So did environmental agencies in Alaska and officials at the pipeline company and at Exxon's headquarters in Houston, Texas.

The spilled oil damaged more than 1,000 miles (1,600 km) of shoreline.

Around 3 a.m. two Coast Guard officers and Dan Lawn of the Alaska Department of Environmental Conservation (DEC) headed out to Bligh Reef. Even before reaching the ship, Lawn could smell the strong, foul odor of the oil. Nearing the *Exxon Valdez*, Lawn saw oil bubbling on the water's surface. Like Ott and other Alaskans who lived in and near Valdez, he had feared that a major oil spill would one day threaten the environment around Prince William Sound. Now it seemed to have happened. But he didn't know what Exxon officials in Houston did. Thanks to computer reports sent directly from the ship, the company realized it was facing the worst oil spill in U.S. history.

While Lawn didn't know the full extent of the spill, he knew that Alyeska was slow to respond. Under contingency plans on file with the Alaska DEC, the company was supposed to send equipment to contain a spill within five hours of an accident. As that deadline

ANOTHER GOOD FRIDAY DISASTER

A tsunami destroyed Valdez's waterfront and a fire swept through the city in March 1964.

Some longtime residents of Valdez woke up on March 24, 1989, and thought back to another tragedy that took place on a Good Friday. Twenty-five years earlier, Good Friday had fallen on March 27. Around 5:30 p.m. that day in 1964, an earthquake centered about 50 miles (80 km) west of Valdez shook the region. On the Richter scale, which was used to measure the strength of earthquakes, the quake registered 9.2—the second most powerful ever recorded anywhere in the world. In some places, buildings shook for more than four minutes.

The effects of the quake were felt across the United States, where it stirred up water in lakes and rivers in almost every state. The earthquake and a tsunami that it caused killed 129 people. In Valdez, the quake destroyed the town's harbor and downtown area. The town was rebuilt on more solid ground. In some places along Prince William Sound, the land rose 38 feet (11.5 m), while in other places it sank 8 feet (2.5 m). In some places where the land went up, the water became too shallow for boats, which meant fishers could no longer work in those waters.

approached, no cleanup ships were in sight. Acting quickly was especially important in this case. Alyeska needed to get the remaining oil off the ship, a process called lightering. With some of the oil already gone, the ship was unevenly balanced on the reef.

The Coast Guard feared that the *Exxon Valdez* could break apart, releasing more oil into the water.

At the Alyeska terminal in Valdez, workers struggled to get the necessary equipment out to the spill site. A barge kept there for cleaning up spills was damaged and out of the water. Snow covered some of the equipment, and workers had to search for it. And only one worker at the terminal that night could drive a forklift, slowing the process of moving equipment onto boats. Lawn called the terminal twice to find out when the equipment was coming. "They told me they were coming, that they had all the stuff coming, and they'd be right out there," he said later. "And we waited, and we waited, and we waited, and we waited."

The first ship to reach the *Exxon Valdez*, carrying lightering equipment, arrived just after noon on March 24. The containment equipment began arriving several hours later. By then the residents of Valdez and surrounding towns knew that something terrible had happened at Bligh Reef. Some of them first heard about the spill from friends and relatives on the East Coast of the United States, where New York-based news stations were reporting about the spill. Alaska Governor Steve Cowper learned about the spill at 7:30 a.m. and quickly left his home in Fairbanks to go to Valdez. Flying over the spill, he thought, "Boy, this is the worst mess I've ever seen."

"Boy, this is the worst mess I've ever seen."

Rescuers held a cormorant covered in oil. Hundreds of thousands of birds were affected by the massive oil spill.

Reporters began to head to Valdez. TV news crews and photographers from around the world also wanted to document the worsening disaster in Prince William Sound. The containment equipment that first reached the site could not stop the spilled oil from spreading, and then bad weather added to the problem. Eventually more than 1,000 miles (1,600 km) of Alaska coastline would be polluted by the oil. Photographs sent from the scene showed dead birds covered with oil and rescue workers trying to clean the oil off animals and rocks on the shore. Those images helped the world understand how the oil spill affected wildlife and people in ways that are still felt today.

ChapterTwo
ALASKA AND ITS OIL

When Europeans first explored Alaska and then settled there, it wasn't oil or fish that attracted them. Russian traders who came to the region during the mid-1700s wanted the furs of land and sea mammals that lived in Alaska and off its coasts. Their focus was on sea otters, seals, beavers, and foxes, and they relied on native hunters to kill the animals and bring them the pelts. At times the Russians traded for the fur, but often they kidnapped native hunters from local communities and forced them to do the work.

The Russians started several small settlements in Alaska to build the fur trade. Indigenous fishers provided most of the seafood the Russians ate. The local people also hunted whales. Other nations were also interested in the furs and whales, including Great Britain, Spain, and the United States. During the 1830s U.S. ships sailed to Alaska to hunt for whales.

The Russians knew the region had gold, though they didn't find enough to make money mining it. Profiting by selling the furs became harder too. By the 1860s the Russian government thought it was too costly to keep its colony in Alaska. In 1867 it sold the land to the United States for $7.2 million. Some Americans saw the purchase as part of the natural, westward growth of the United States. They also realized that this

Native Alaskans sold furs, seafood, and whales to Russian traders during the 18th and 19th centuries.

area, which was twice the size of Texas, had valuable resources. But others made fun of U.S. Secretary of State William Seward, who had arranged the purchase from Russia. They called the deal "Seward's Folly" and thought the government had wasted money buying a remote piece of land. The actual cost eventually would be even higher because the United States would have to send soldiers there to defend it.

One supporter of the purchase was Perry Collins, who had once proposed putting a telegraph line through Alaska to link North America and Russia. *The New York Times* published a letter he wrote to Secretary Seward praising Alaska and its resources. Collins wrote, "The fisheries alone are worth more than the whole cost of the country, and will repay us in the future amply for the investment." Collins wanted Seward and others to see that "the country of Russian-America cannot be considered, as some would have it, a dreary waste of glaciers, icebergs, white bears and walrus."

After the purchase, Americans came to Alaska to hunt, fish, and mine. The miners eventually tapped into the gold there, and the fishers created an industry around the catching and canning of salmon. By 1917 the Alaska Territory had more than 100 canneries. Later, fishers also caught and canned large amounts of crab. But in the 20th century, oil became Alaska's most valuable natural resource.

Native Alaskans and Russian settlers had noticed places where oil from underground oozed up to the surface. In 1902 the Alaska Development Company drilled Alaska's first commercial oil well in Katalla, not far from Cordova. The region was already home to several coal mines. Over the next several decades, some oil was brought to the surface there, but the U.S. government limited how much land could be

.......3625. New Metlakahtla, Indian Salmon Cannery.

A stereographic image taken in 1890 of an Alaskan salmon cannery was made to be seen through a special viewer. The image would seem to appear in 3-D.

sold for oil exploration and coal mining. President Theodore Roosevelt, in particular, wanted the natural resources to belong to the country and not be sold to private companies.

Oil seeps like the ones in Katalla also occurred much farther north, in Alaska's Arctic region. The U.S. Navy owned land in Alaska that was known to hold vast amounts of petroleum and natural gas. The area, which is near the Arctic Ocean, is known as the North Slope. But since working in distant and frigid Alaska was costly, the Navy never authorized drilling for oil there.

After World War II, oil companies once again became interested in searching for Alaskan oil.

They had better methods for finding potential wells, and world events made them eager to explore U.S. lands. Drilling for oil in foreign countries could be risky. The foreign governments could restrict their activities or even shut down the oil operations, and U.S. relations with the countries could turn from friendly to hostile very quickly.

The discovery of new oil fields during the 1950s began Alaska's real oil boom. Even before the first major strike in 1957, Alaska's government leaders were counting on making money from oil. In 1955 the territorial legislature passed a 1 percent tax on the value of all oil and natural gas produced in the territory.

Alaska did not remain a territory for long. Congress voted in 1958 to let Alaska enter the Union as the 49th state. Alaska officially became a state in January 1959. U.S. officials knew that oil and natural gas production would become an important part of the state's economy. At the time, though, fishing was still Alaska's most important industry.

Under the law that made Alaska a state, it could claim ownership of more than 100 million acres (40 million hectares) of land that had belonged to the federal government. Some of the land claimed by Alaska's leaders was in the North Slope, around Prudhoe Bay. The state took this land knowing that it could become an important source of oil, which would bring a lot of money to the state.

Oil drilling was important to the Alaska economy even before statehood in 1959.

Even before major exploration of Prudhoe Bay began in 1968, oil played an ever-growing role in the state's economy. In 1967 Alaska's share of the nation's total oil and gas production was worth more money than the state's fisheries. At the end of that year, the oil company Atlantic-Richfield, now called Arco, struck oil in Prudhoe Bay. Natural gas streamed out of the well (the gas and petroleum are often found together). The oil that Atlantic-Richfield had discovered came from the largest oil field ever found in North America. Experts estimated that it held 25 billion barrels of oil.

Other oil companies joined Atlantic-Richfield in exploring the area. They knew they controlled huge amounts of oil, but they weren't sure how to get it to refineries along the Pacific coast. Humble Oil, which later became Exxon, considered shipping it by sea from the Arctic Ocean and around Alaska's western coast. Getting through the Arctic ice, however, proved too hard. Some people talked about building a pipeline into Canada and then into the Midwest of the United States. Critics of that idea did not like the idea that a foreign country—even a friendly one—would have some control over the flow of American oil. Finally the companies made plans for the Trans-Alaska Pipeline System, proposing to build an underground pipeline from the oil fields to Valdez. The port was warm enough to remain ice-free all year long.

Before construction began, however, several tribes went to court to prevent it from being built. In 1966 indigenous Alaskans had created the Alaska Federation of Natives to assert their rights and land claims. The tribes wanted the U.S. government to return lands they said had been taken from them. The state of Alaska and the indigenous tribes sometimes had conflicting land claims. With the plans for the new pipeline, the native people worried that oil spills could pollute rivers and streams on land they considered theirs.

The court battle between the indigenous people and both Alaska and the United States led Congress in 1971 to pass the Alaska Native Claims Settlement Act. Under the law, the tribes received 44 million acres (18 million hectares) of land and almost $1 billion. Some of the money would come from the future production of oil. The law also called on the U.S. government to decide which federally owned Alaskan lands should be set aside to protect wildlife. Alaska's nickname is "The Last Frontier," and many Americans across the country wanted to preserve as much of its natural beauty as possible.

Tourists and residents alike want to safeguard Alaska's beauty, including Denali National Park.

Even with the land claims settlement, the oil companies still could not start building the pipeline system. Environmental groups raised legal issues that they said the companies had not addressed. Among those with environmental concerns were fishers on Prince William Sound, especially in Cordova. They worried that an oil spill could hurt their businesses, which they relied on to feed their families. Some of the fishers pushed for the pipeline through Canada. But many more Alaskans supported the pipeline to Valdez and the jobs it would bring to the state.

Finally, in 1973, Congress amended a law that fishers and environmentalists were using to try to stop the pipeline. With that change, the legal requirements for building the pipeline had been met. In November, President Richard Nixon signed the law that let the building begin. By then the country was in the middle of a gasoline crisis. Major suppliers of oil in the Middle East had stopped sending it to the United States, and the price of gas for cars skyrocketed. Supporters of the Alaska pipeline saw it as a way to reduce America's need to import oil.

Nixon had promised Alaska's fishers and Congress that new ships with double hulls would carry the oil out of Valdez. The second hull would make it harder for oil to spill if a ship ran aground. The government said the ships would also separate seawater used as ballast from the holds

MONEY FOR ALASKA'S RESIDENTS

Alaska residents process their dividend applications at an office in downtown Anchorage.

Before the first drop of oil flowed through the Trans-Alaska Pipeline System, Alaska voters decided they wanted to make sure the state saved and wisely used the money it earned from oil. In 1976 the voters approved the creation of what was called a Permanent Fund.

Part of the money made from the sale of the state's oil and mineral resources would go into the fund. By investing this money, the state would make more money. The principal, the amount taken in from the natural resources, could never be spent, but the money made from the investments could.

Most of that money has been used to pay a dividend to Alaska residents. With only a few exceptions, any legal resident of the state can claim a dividend—even children. The first dividend checks went out in 1982, with each Alaskan earning $1,000. The amount of the dividend rises and falls, but Alaskans have received money from oil every year since that first dividend.

that contained oil. That way, when the ballast was released into Prince William Sound, it wouldn't pollute the waters. In the end, however, the oil companies were not forced to meet the promises the government made.

Construction of the pipeline began in 1975, using sections of steel pipe 4 feet (1.2 m) wide. Oil comes

The Trans-Alaska pipeline snakes above the ground in parts of its 800-mile (1,287-km) journey from Prudhoe Bay to Valdez.

out of the ground at a temperature of 180 degrees Fahrenheit (82 degrees Celsius). In some places, the hot oil flowing through such a pipe underground would have heated the frozen ground enough to make the pipe unstable. So the pipe could not go under the surface in those areas. But putting it on the surface would have disrupted the movement of caribou herds. The solution was to raise sections of the pipeline off the ground so the caribou could pass underneath. It took just over two years to finish, at a cost of $8 billion, and 70,000 workers took part in the project. The first tanker carrying Prudhoe Bay oil left Valdez on August 1, 1977.

As the tankers began to sail in and out of Valdez, the oil companies looked for ways to cut their costs.

They had already persuaded the U.S. government to let them use single-hull ships instead of ships with two hulls. Then they sought to cut back on some safety measures, also to save money. The minimum number of crew needed to run a ship was reduced, and harbor pilots were not required to have as much training as the Coast Guard recommended. Alaska passed some laws to address safety and environmental concerns, but in general state leaders went along with the oil companies. Oil was making the state rich; in 1982 alone the state earned more than $4 billion in taxes and royalties.

Despite their earlier concerns, Alaska fishers were also making money. The number of fish caught and their value changed from year to year, but 1988 was a good year, especially for salmon fishers. They brought in fish worth more than $700 million—about $100 million more than the year before. Fishing's economic value to Alaska was second only to that of the oil industry. Some of the salmon came from state hatcheries, while other hatcheries were operated by private groups.

Riki Ott and her partner, Danny Carpenter, were among the Cordova fishers who celebrated their success in 1988. Ott later wrote, "We could afford to play for the winter. We could afford anything, it seemed." The two took a vacation in Hawaii, and Carpenter quit his winter job. Ott and other local fishers looked forward to another good season in 1989—until the grounding of the *Exxon Valdez* crushed that hope.

ChapterThree
THE SLOW CLEANUP

On the evening of March 24, 1989, the day of the spill, Valdez residents gathered in the Valdez Civic Center to hear Frank Iarossi talk about the accident. Iarossi was the president of Exxon Shipping, and Exxon, not Alyeska, would take charge of the cleanup. By that afternoon, the oil slick coming from the *Exxon Valdez* was several miles long.

Under the contingency plan it had filed with Alaska, Alyeska was supposed to be in charge of a cleanup after an oil spill. Although Alyeska did not have the equipment nearby to contain and clean up the spill, Exxon's taking charge posed some problems. The effort would now be directed from Houston, not locally, and, as even Iarossi admitted, the company had no system for dealing with a spill of this size. But he also said that the company had told the state several years before that if an Exxon ship was involved in a major spill, Exxon would take charge of the cleanup. Later, Dennis Kelso, head of Alaska's Department of Environmental Conservation, criticized Exxon for taking control of the cleanup efforts. "In the process," he said, "fishermen and other knowledgeable locals were left out."

Speaking to representatives of the news media, Iarossi explained what the company had already

The *Exxon Valdez* remained in place after it ran aground on a reef in Prince William Sound.

done. Two of its tankers were on the way to Valdez to lighter the oil still on the *Exxon Valdez*. The company was also assembling cleanup teams and bringing in oil-spill experts. Iarossi discussed using chemicals called dispersants to break up the oil in the water. Once broken into small droplets, the oil would sink into the water, rather than being washed ashore.

The Alyeska contingency plan called for the possible use of dispersants, but a test that afternoon had not gone well. The chemical works best when the water is moving slightly, but the water in Prince William Sound that day was calm. Even if the dispersants worked, there were not enough available to deal with a spill of this size.

At the Valdez community meeting, when Iarossi discussed using dispersants, Riki Ott spoke up. She mentioned her background in marine science and then pointed out that the dispersed oil droplets, when they sank, could harm fish in the water. Local fishers, she said, were very concerned about the harmful effects of the chemicals on their future earnings. And the contingency plan, state officials knew, called for using dispersant chemicals only as a last resort, after mechanical methods to contain and remove the oil had failed.

The mechanical tools included floating barriers called booms, which kept the oil from spreading, and skimmers, which removed the oil from the water. The equipment Alyeska had on hand in Valdez could not begin to clean up a spill the size of the one near Bligh Reef. More equipment began arriving on Saturday morning, but it was still not enough to do the job. Iarossi continued to press for using dispersants. He said on Sunday that mechanical methods would not "do the job. … It is the slowest and least effective tool." Exxon also suggested burning off the oil, but a test showed that the smoke from the burning fuel posed a health hazard to residents of a nearby

Environmental activist Riki Ott has written two books on the consequences of the *Exxon Valdez* oil spill.

Booms were used to prevent spilled oil from spreading in Alaska's waters.

indigenous village. Some local residents believed that Exxon was more concerned about making the spilled oil disappear than about taking into account the long-term effects of the spill on people and the environment.

By Sunday morning, Exxon had managed to remove only 126,000 gallons (476,962 liters) of oil—much less than the contingency plan called for within two days of a spill. By then, Exxon had announced that almost 11 million gallons (42 million liters) had poured into Prince William Sound.

The cleanup had been going slowly under what were ideal weather conditions for a mechanical cleanup. The shortage of equipment, though, had slowed the process. Now nature stepped in to turn a horrible spill in the sound into a disaster that affected about 1,300 miles (2,092 km) of Alaska coastline. On Easter Sunday night, a strong storm hit Prince William Sound. Winds of more than 70 miles (113 km) per hour pushed waves up to 20 feet (6 m) high. When residents awoke the next day, they saw that in some places the wind had blown the oil from 30 to 40 feet (9 to 12 m) up off the ground and into trees. Oil had moved 40 miles (64 km) from the crash site, and the wind had whipped the oil and seawater into a mixture called mousse. The mousse would be harder to clean up than the oil itself, and dispersants would not work on the mixture. With the chance for containing the spill gone, oil would eventually drift more than 500 miles (805 km) from where the *Exxon Valdez* went aground.

Flying above the scene, fishers of Valdez and Cordova saw oil covering many beaches, with dead and dying birds and sea otters covered in the black goo.

Oil from the spill covered miles and miles of Alaska's beaches.

Some fishers, including Ott, told Exxon officials about the danger the spreading oil posed to other beaches and fish hatcheries. But Exxon was not prepared to handle the movement of oil that followed, as wind and currents took it all over the Alaska coast.

As more cleanup equipment slowly reached the area, some local fishers took their own steps to fight the spill. In early April, Tom Copeland and a few friends went out in a boat with a pump and buckets. They began filling the buckets with the spilled oil. Exxon had booms in the area holding back oil, but

The *Exxon Valdez* was refloated and towed away from Bligh Reef nearly two weeks after the accident.

no skimmers to pick it up. Despite the fact that Copeland and his friends successfully picked up some oil, Exxon officials in the region told them to leave. So the fishers headed to another spot with oil—and no Exxon workers. On the first day, Copeland and his team picked up 500 gallons (1,893 liters) of oil. It was just a drop compared with the millions of gallons in the water. But on at least one day, the fishers picked up more oil than Exxon's skimmers did. As Copeland later said, "It was the most magnificent feeling, to actually be putting a

"It was the most magnificent feeling, to actually be putting a dent in this disaster. Since then I have never doubted the power of the individual to change things."

dent in this disaster. Since then I have never doubted the power of the individual to change things."

Other local residents tried to spur Exxon to act more quickly. One problem was protecting the hatcheries. At a public meeting, fisher Michelle Hahn O'Leary explained that the company's floating barrier booms were designed for harbor spills, not ones in open water. But the company was not trying to get the necessary booms. "We can't seem to get it through Exxon," O'Leary said. "Exxon can't deliver."

Later in the spring, O'Leary went to Washington, D.C., to speak to Congress about the spill. She said everyone seemed surprised that such a spill had happened, but she said fishers and some Alaska officials had warned about the dangers of a major spill even before the pipeline construction had begun. One Alaska lawmaker had even predicted that a spill could happen at Bligh Reef.

Exxon eventually brought in thousands of workers to help with the cleanup. It also hired local fishers to help with the effort. Some residents of Valdez and Cordova welcomed the chance to earn money, especially since they could no longer fish in the sound. Others, however, were so angry with Exxon that they refused to work for the company. Money flowed into the region, thanks to Exxon, creating what some people called "spillionaires." The nickname was meant as an insult—people who were angry with Exxon grew disgusted with some of the people helping the company. Exxon paid higher wages than local businesses did, and some struggled to stay open as their employees left to work for Exxon. But even with Exxon's cash coming into the region, Alaskans along the sound took a huge financial loss. Fishers could not fish, and businesses that supplied them suffered as well. Even salmon fishers far from the sound were affected. People outside the state were reluctant to buy Alaskan salmon that year, fearing it might somehow be tainted by oil.

The population of Valdez almost quadrupled as cleanup workers poured in. Many began using high-powered hoses to wash oil off rocks. Some had only rags to clean off the rocks. Later some workers used a chemical designed to break up the oil on the rocks without harming the environment. The workers' efforts, however, were sometimes wasted, as the tide brought more oil onto the shore and the chemical did not affect oil under the rocks. In addition, the hot water from the hoses destroyed some of the shellfish and plant life that hadn't been affected by the oil. The water also created a fine spray filled with oil that covered the workers. They wore raincoats, but sometimes took them off, getting the spray on their exposed skin. The workers breathed the oil spray as well.

Workers used pressure washers in an attempt to rinse oil from beaches.

Seeing that the cleanup on shore wasn't as effective as Alaskans had hoped, Coast Guard officer Clyde Robbins and others wondered whether it was worth the effort. Robbins later recalled that some people running the cleanup thought "that we might be better doing nothing and letting Mother Nature take care of it. But doing nothing wasn't an option, ever. We had to do something, even if it was just looking busy."

A veterinarian in Alaska examined a sick deer, which became ill after the *Exxon Valdez* accident.

Volunteers and paid workers tried to rescue birds and other animals that had been soaked in oil. Some animals weren't touched by the oil but were still affected by it. About 300 miles (483 km) away from the spill site, people found deer and bear

"At least
once or twice
a day, you
had to just
sit down
and weep."

that had died from eating oil-covered seaweed. Even the cleanup process posed problems. Being cleaned by well-meaning humans using a dishwashing liquid was hard on the animals, and some animals that had been covered with oil returned to the wild carrying diseases. The work was hard for some of the rescuers too. Kelley Weaverling, a guide from Cordova, remembered how he and the other rescuers were affected by seeing dead animals. "At least once or twice a day," he said, "you had to just sit down and weep."

Exxon knew that people across the country were angry about the spill and how it had affected such a beautiful part of the country. Some people who had regularly bought Exxon gas began cutting up the company's credit cards. Exxon wanted Americans to think it was doing everything it could to clean up the spill as quickly as possible. It presented the best side of the cleanup effort to the news media. Alaska officials, however, knew that what Exxon reported was not always true. The state worked hard to make sure that journalists could see for themselves the damage the spill had done, and continued to do, as more animals were killed.

One photojournalist didn't have far to go to cover the *Exxon Valdez* story. Photographer Bob Hallinen was working for the *Anchorage Daily News*, the newspaper in Alaska's largest city. He first arrived in

Cordova to photograph a meeting with residents, state officials, and representatives from Exxon. "It was supposed to be an overnight trip," he said. "A month later, I returned home."

During that month, Hallinen documented the efforts to clean wildlife and remove oil from the coast. Working before digital cameras became available, he used two cameras that shot film used to make slides. He traveled with Weaverling and other rescuers, spending nights on a tour boat that served as a floating hotel. Hallinen later recalled that he spent "weeks with the boats photographing the capturing of oiled birds and sea otters. Every day the crew would take skiffs to the beach and walk the shoreline of islands in the sound looking for oiled wildlife." To get the film developed, the captain of whatever boat Hallinen was on would radio other boats heading to Valdez. In town, someone from the returning boat or a reporter or photographer there would take the film to the airport to get it to Anchorage for processing.

Hallinen then used Valdez as his base as he worked with reporters covering particular stories related to the oil spill. He took pictures that illustrated their words. At times he took helicopters out along the sound to photograph the cleanup work on the island beaches. He recalled photographing state scientists, who "would wipe off oil from the birds and

Bob Hallinen of the *Anchorage Daily News* photographed workers using high-pressure hoses to blast oil from a beach in Prince William Sound.

examine them to catalog the wildlife killed in the spill." Hallinen's photos were distributed across the country by the Associated Press, which provides news and photos to newspapers and other news organizations around the world.

As the cleanup went on, Exxon and government officials tried to learn what had caused the accident on March 24. That night, several people had smelled alcohol on Captain Joseph Hazelwood's breath, and he had been seen drinking the day before in Valdez. When his blood was tested 10 hours after the crash, he was legally drunk, based on the limits the Coast Guard had set for ships' captains. Exxon knew Hazelwood had a history of alcohol-related problems. But government officials couldn't say whether the alcohol in his blood was from before or after the crash. While Hazelwood wasn't commanding the ship when it happened, he had broken rules by turning the *Exxon Valdez* over to third mate Gregory Cousins, who was not licensed to pilot the ship in the sound. Cousins had worked many hours without much sleep before taking command. The Coast Guard also received some blame for using old equipment to keep track of the ships in Prince William Sound.

With the news of Hazelwood's drinking, the state of Alaska filed legal charges against him. During the summer, the state also sued Exxon and Alyeska, and Exxon faced lawsuits from private citizens as well. The cleanup went on through the summer of 1989, with no one knowing what the long-term effects of the spill would be.

THE CAPTAIN IN COURT

Former Exxon Valdez *captain Joseph Hazelwood performed community service in an Anchorage café.*

After the results of Joseph Hazelwood's alcohol test, Exxon fired him, and the state charged him with four crimes, including operating a ship while drunk. If he had been found guilty of all charges, Hazelwood would have faced up to seven years in prison and fines of more than $60,000. His trial began in January 1990 and lasted for about eight weeks. In the end, the jury decided that he was not drunk at the time of the grounding, though it did find him guilty of a lesser charge. The verdict was announced two days before the first anniversary of the accident.

Hazelwood appealed the decision and lost, so he had to pay a fine and do 1,000 hours of unpaid work, known as community service. He left his home in New York and spent most of the time working at an Anchorage café that gives homeless people free food. His duties included cleaning stoves and waxing floors.

"I was the captain of a ship that ran aground and caused a horrendous amount of damage," said Hazelwood, almost 20 years after the spill. "I've got to be responsible for that." He also offered "an apology, a very heartfelt apology, to the people of Alaska for the damage caused by the grounding of a ship that I was in command of."

ChapterFour
AFTERMATH OF A DISASTER

Exxon announced in mid-September 1989 that it was ending the cleanup process for the year. Although Exxon was pulling out, Alaska state officials continued cleaning up on their own as best as they could through the winter. They were helped by winter storms that pushed some of the remaining oil away from the coast. In 1990 fewer workers went to the coast for the ongoing cleanup effort than the year before. But as people discovered, large amounts of oil remained under rocks and sand. Even so, Exxon claimed in the fall of 1990 that areas affected by the spill "are healing rapidly" and "the water is pure." Riki Ott called this "nonsense." She and others believed the truth about the extent of the damage had not reached the public.

Before Exxon ended its cleanup work in Valdez, local fishers and environmentalists vented some of the anger they still felt toward the giant oil company. As another tanker sat in the harbor taking on oil, a small fleet of fishing boats and other vessels paraded in front of it. The protesters raised banners saying "Give Us Back Alaska! No More Oil Lies" and "Plan for the Future!"

The fishers of Prince William Sound lost an estimated $50 million because of the spill. Along

A parade of fishing boats protested in the waters near Valdez in September 1989.

with financial losses, more than 6,000 cleanup workers suffered health problems because of their exposure to the oily mist created when the oil was sprayed off rocks. Some workers developed breathing problems or felt as if they had the flu. Local people called the ailments the "Valdez crud," and some suffered the effects for years. A few sued Exxon, saying the company knew they faced health risks but did not give them proper protection.

Exxon thought it had acted responsibly after the spill. From the beginning, it had promised to pay for any financial losses local residents suffered. The company paid a total of $2.5 billion to try to clean up the sound. Affected residents filed more than 32,000 claims with Exxon to try to collect money from the company. Others filed lawsuits, seeking greater payments than Exxon was willing to pay.

Even before the legal cases began, the U.S. government wanted to understand what had caused the worst oil spill in the country's history. In May 1989 President George H. W. Bush received a report on the accident—the first of several from federal and state agencies. The report said that both the oil companies and government agencies had not prepared properly for a spill the size of the one in Prince William Sound. For the future, the report said in part, "Steps must be taken to improve overall planning for, and care of, wildlife affected by oil spills."

Another key report came in February 1990 from the Alaska Oil Spill Commission. The commission harshly criticized oil companies like Exxon, which had ignored safety rules set down in the 1970s in order to make more money. The Coast Guard was part of the problem too, because it did not enforce the rules. The report added that "all parties, the shippers, Alyeska, the Coast Guard and the State of Alaska" had roles to play in preventing spills like the one that

As part of the cleanup effort, a plane sprayed chemicals on the oil spill three days after the accident. Reports after the spill placed blame on oil companies and government agencies.

polluted Prince William Sound and beyond. But after going more than a decade without a major accident, the parties felt confident that one would never happen. That confidence played a role in their not properly following and enforcing safety rules.

The Alaska report also called for something the government had promised years before—tankers with double hulls. In 1990 Congress passed a law to ensure that the ships had the hulls and that other safety measures were added for transporting oil. The Oil Pollution Act said shippers could use their existing single-hull ships, but new ones had to have the second hull. The law also called for new rules to keep sailors from working too long, so they wouldn't get tired. And people who had lost their license because of drunken driving—as Joseph Hazelwood had before 1989—could not get a captain's license. In addition, the law created a tax to set up a fund to help pay for future spills. Congress also created the Oil Spill Recovery Institute (OSRI). Its duties included studying how to prevent spills in the area and measuring the impact of the *Exxon Valdez* spill on Prince William Sound.

As the cleanup continued in Alaska, the U.S. government, the state, and individuals pursued their lawsuits against Exxon. One legal settlement came in 1991. Exxon agreed to plead guilty to four minor crimes and pay $125 million in fines. The company also promised to pay $900 million over 10 years to help with future cleanup efforts in Prince William Sound. Alaska had the right to ask for more money if that amount didn't cover future cleanup costs.

By agreeing to this deal, Exxon also agreed to drop its own lawsuit against Alaska. The company wanted the state to pay for damages caused by the spill. Exxon claimed the state should have let it use chemical dispersants, as it had wanted, soon after the spill. Exxon also continued to put the blame for the accident on Hazelwood, ignoring the broader range of reasons the government reports had cited.

GOING TO DOUBLE-HULL SHIPS

A double-hull oil tanker maneuvered through a lock in Ontario, Canada.

Beginning in 2015, U.S. law said tankers with only one hull could no longer carry oil in U.S. waters. Many companies had already switched to double-hull ships before then. An international organization that oversees shipping had set an earlier deadline for companies to switch to double-hull tankers.

The second hull puts a second layer of steel between the seawater and the oil carried inside a ship's first hull. The oil is not kept in barrels or other containers; it is poured directly into the holds. A double hull can't prevent all oil spills, but it can reduce the amount of oil spilled. And it can lower the chance that one

will happen. That was the case in 2009, when the double-hull Norwegian tanker *Satilla* collided with a damaged oil rig that had sunk in the Gulf of Mexico. Such rigs pump oil from beneath the floor of the ocean.

The *Satilla* was carrying 41 million gallons (155 million liters) of oil when the accident occurred, but none of it spilled into the water. Dennis Kelso, who worked for the Alaska Department of Environmental Conservation in 1989, praised the double-hull construction of the *Satilla*. "This could have been a serious spill. Because of that double hull that suffered damage on its exterior, there was no oil spill at all."

After the oil spill, a boom protected a stream that flowed into Prince William Sound. The stream was vital to salmon survival.

Alaskans with their own lawsuits still wanted more from Exxon. In 1993, the company denied that the spill had had anything to do with a poor season for Prince William Sound fishers. The herring industry had been almost wiped out since the spill, and that year, the salmon catch was worth only $5 million. The fishers wanted Exxon to keep its promise to pay for any damages they had suffered because of the spill. Some fishers used their boats to block the entry to the port in Valdez, keeping out oil tankers for several days. Government officials tried to persuade Exxon to make a deal with the fishers, but the company refused to talk to them. Hundreds of lawyers on both sides prepared for a court trial in case Exxon and the fishers could not reach an agreement.

The two sides failed to settle out of court, and the trial began in Anchorage on May 2, 1994. Both sides brought in experienced—and expensive—lawyers. Together, the two sides spent several hundred million dollars preparing for their day in court. The trial lasted until June 13, when the jury announced its verdict. Exxon, the jury said, had been negligent—it had not done things it should have done to avoid the spill. The company was also found to be reckless in letting Hazelwood command the *Exxon Valdez*, given his past problems with alcohol.

Exxon had already agreed that it had been negligent and would pay some money to thousands of Prince William Sound residents who had been affected by the spill. But Exxon thought the $1.5 billion the fishers sought was too high. And now, with the verdict of acting recklessly, Exxon also faced punitive damages—payments meant to punish the company for its actions. The Alaska residents wanted $15 billion in punitive damages. "A company as large as Exxon thinks that it is above the law," said their lead attorney, Brian O'Neill. "You need to take a substantial bite out of their butt before they change their behavior. This verdict will help to do that and send a message to all the Exxons of the world."

Exxon thought that amount was much too high, and one of its attorneys, Patrick Lynch, defended the company. "Exxon's behavior after the accident was exemplary. We took extraordinary steps to clean up, to compensate people, and to correct and improve operating practices."

The second phase of the trial then began, with the jury deciding exactly how much Exxon would pay. The amounts awarded were $287 million to pay for what the residents lost and $5 billion in punitive damages. Exxon appealed the decision, and the case remained in the courts for another 14 years. Finally, in 2008, the U.S. Supreme Court agreed with Exxon

A group from Kodiak, Alaska, protested in front of the Supreme Court in 2008.

that the punitive award was too high. Exxon had to pay only $507.5 million in punitive damages.

Because of the long court battle, several thousand Alaska fishers died before they received all the money they were due. Others struggled with debt as they tried to make a living in waters still affected by the spill. The value of the permits the fishers had to buy before they could fish also fell. In good years, fishers could sell their permits to other fishers for more than what they had paid for them. In 1988 a salmon permit was worth about $250,000. By 2007 the same permit was worth less than $50,000.

Photographers, including Bob Hallinen, had shown the world the damage the oil did to wildlife and the coastline. But no pictures captured the effect of the spill on the people of Prince William Sound. In August 1989 researchers Duane Gill and Steve Picou interviewed residents of Cordova to see how the spill affected them personally. The two did more interviews over the next seven years. They learned that many residents suffered from depression and other emotional problems, especially if they had relied on fishing in the sound to make a living. Drug and alcohol abuse rose, as did suicides.

Gill and Picou saw a difference between natural disasters—like the 1964 earthquake and tsunami that devastated the region—and what they called technological disasters. With natural disasters, Gill said, "usually people pull together and rebuild their community. After a year or two, you might not even know anything had happened." But with technological disasters, "people might not agree on how to respond or recover." The long court battle made it hard for residents to put the spill behind them. Gill added, "And as long as you go out on the sound and don't see or hear many birds and marine life, the disaster is still happening."

Scientists have tried to determine the lasting effects of the spill on the wildlife of Prince William Sound. The number of herring never returned to pre-spill levels, but the scientists think other factors besides oil played a part. A 2017 report said the other factors could include the addition of fresh water to the sound's salt water, caused by melting glaciers. The melting is linked to the global warming that scientists have pointed out for decades. Another study in 2017 said melting glaciers also could have played a role in the 1989 spill. Just after TAPS opened in 1977, some scientists warned that rising temperatures could create more icebergs from glaciers. The icebergs could affect shipping lanes in Alaska. And on March 23, 1989, icebergs had forced the *Exxon Valdez* out of its usual path just before the accident.

With birds and sea mammals, the spill played a more direct role. Wildlife died because they ate food covered with oil, or oil on their fur or feathers prevented that outer layer from keeping the animals warm, as fur and feathers are supposed to do. The animals then died from

"And as long as you go out on the sound and don't see or hear many birds and marine life, the disaster is still happening."

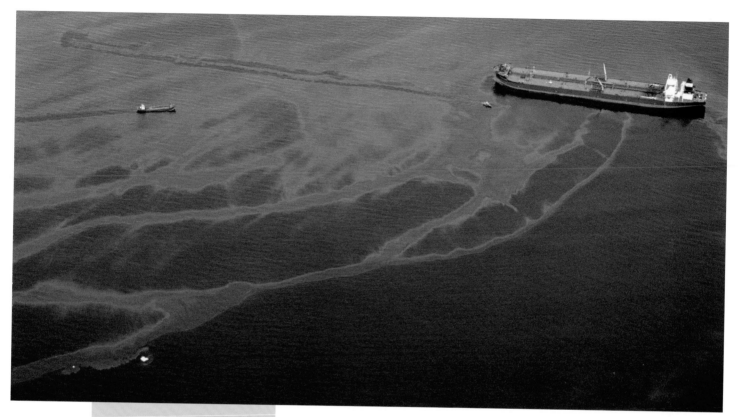

The *Exxon Valdez* oil spill had dramatic effects on people, wildlife, and the environment.

exposure to cold weather and water. Some animals did not die directly from oil, but they might not have been healthy enough to avoid being killed by other animals. By one estimate reported by the state of Alaska, the spill killed 250,000 seabirds, almost 3,000 sea otters, 250 bald eagles, and almost two dozen orcas.

Scientists have reported some good news. The number of sea otters and harlequin ducks seemed to have returned to their pre-spill levels by 2013. And the spill helped scientists learn more about the effects of even small amounts of oil on some wildlife. U.S. government scientist Dan Esler said in 2014, "The understanding that lingering in oil could have chronic effects on wildlife populations was a new and important finding, and one that we did not anticipate at the time that we started the research." Of course, that knowledge came at huge cost to the fish, birds, and mammals affected by the spill.

Today oil from the *Exxon Valdez* can still be found on parts of the Alaska coast. Exxon, which has since merged with the oil company Mobil, calls the spill "one of the lowest points in ExxonMobil's 125-year history." And despite the Oil Pollution Act of 1990, other oil spills have taken place. Some environmentalists want oil companies to contribute more to a fund set up to pay for damages for spills. Others say the technology for cleaning up spills has not improved much since 1989. Having a contingency plan is not helpful if it can't be effectively carried out.

For their work documenting the *Exxon Valdez* spill, Bob Hallinen and two other photographers from the *Anchorage Daily News*—Erik Hill and Paul Souders—were finalists for the 1990 Pulitzer Prize for feature photography. The Pulitzer Prizes are the highest honor in U.S. journalism. Hallinen said, "It was fun for a while to think that we would be a Pulitzer winner. But even to be one of the finalists for a Pulitzer is a great honor and I am proud of the work that my fellow photographers … and I did to document the *Exxon Valdez* oil spill."

Decades after photographing the spill, Hallinen was still affected by what he saw. "Prince William

Bob Hallinen's heartbreaking photo of a worker trying to clean an oil-covered bird helped show the world the effects of the 1989 oil spill.

Sound looks like it did before the spill but it seems that there are still lingering effects," he said in 2017. "Having been out on Prince William Sound before the spill and seeing the effects of the oil on the wildlife and the beaches was heartbreaking. The sound is an incredibly beautiful place and seeing it devastated by the oil spill was hard to witness."

Some of Hallinen's pictures still appear on websites and in newspapers. They remind the world about the potential dangers of a major oil spill to wildlife and the communities affected by this kind of disaster.

Timeline

1867

The United States buys Alaska from Russia for $7.2 million

1902

The first commercial oil well is drilled in Alaska

March 27, 1964

An earthquake and tsunami devastate Valdez and Alaska

1967

The Atlantic-Richfield Company discovers oil on Alaska's North Slope

1955

The Alaska legislature passes a tax on oil drilled there

1959

Alaska becomes the 49th state

1975

Construction begins on the Trans-Alaska Pipeline System, which will bring oil from the North Slope to the port at Valdez

1977

The first oil tanker sails from Valdez

Timeline

1982

For the first time, Alaskans receive money from the state's Permanent Fund, paid for by money the state received from oil production

March 24, 1989

The *Exxon Valdez* runs aground in Prince William Sound and millions of gallons of oil begin spilling from the ship

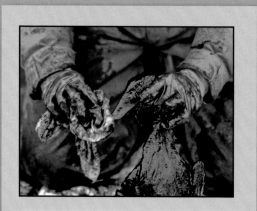

1991

Exxon pleads guilty to four criminal charges for its role in the oil spill and agrees to pay more than $1 billion, on top of what it had already spent for cleanup efforts

1994

A jury finds that Exxon was both negligent and reckless and calls for the company to pay more than $5 billion in punitive damages; Exxon appeals the decision

March 26, 1989

A strong storm pushes some of the oil out of the sound

1990

Joseph Hazelwood, captain of the *Exxon Valdez*, is found guilty of negligence; Congress passes the Oil Pollution Act to try to reduce the risk of future major oil spills

2008

The U.S. Supreme Court reduces the punitive damages Exxon must pay to just over $500 million

2014

The National Oceanic and Atmospheric Administration reports that most of the species affected by the oil spill have recovered, but Prince William Sound has not fully returned to pre-spill conditions

Glossary

aground—stuck on land or on the bottom of a body of water

amended—changed using a specific legal process

ballast—weight added to a ship to help keep it stable at sea

bridge—the control center of a ship

chronic—lasting for a long time

contingency plan—steps that will be taken in case an emergency occurs

dispersant—liquid or gas used to uniformly distribute small particles

hatchery—place where the hatching of fish eggs is carefully controlled so the fish can be released into the wild

hold—area of ship used to store cargo

indigenous—native to a place

legislature—the branch of a government that makes laws

marine—related to the sea

petroleum—raw material for fuel oil that is found under the ground and processed into a variety of chemicals, including gasoline, kerosene, and natural gas

pilot—person with expert local knowledge who takes charge of a ship entering or leaving a harbor

refinery—place where petroleum is made into gasoline, motor oil, and other products

tsunami—gigantic ocean wave created by an undersea earthquake, landslide, or volcanic eruption

Additional Resources

Further Reading

Bogart, Jon. *Animals and Oil Spills.*
New York: Gareth Stevens Publishing, 2014.

Scherer, Lauri S., ed. *Oil.*
Detroit: Greenhaven Press, 2013.

Wang, Andrea. *The Science of an Oil Spill.*
Ann Arbor, Mich.: Cherry Lake Publishing, 2015.

Internet Sites

Use FactHound to find Internet sites
related to this book.
Visit *www.facthound.com*
Just type in 9780756557430 and go.

Critical Thinking Questions

Why did some fishers and indigenous Alaskans oppose the building of the Trans-Alaska pipeline? Which group or groups of people do you think had the most to lose by an oil spill and why?

During the early 1970s, why were U.S. lawmakers eager to drill for oil in the United States? Do you think oil drilling within the U.S. is a good idea? Why or why not?

In what ways did Exxon fail to meet the contingency plan that was in place at the time of the *Exxon Valdez* accident? Use examples from the text to support your answer.

Source Notes

Page 6, line 19: Riki Ott. *Not One Drop: Betrayal and Courage in the Wake of the Exxon Valdez Oil Spill.* White River Junction, Vt.: Chelsea Green Publishing, 2008, p. 38.

Page 6, line 21: Carey Restino. "Recalling the shock and sadness of Exxon Valdez spill 25 years ago." *Alaska Dispatch News.* 22 March 2014. Updated 28 Sept. 2016. 26 Sept. 2017. https://www.adn.com/alaska-news/article/recalling-shock-and-sadness-exxon-valdez-spill-25-years-ago/2014/03/23/

Page 8, line 21: Angela Day. *Red Light to Starboard: Recalling the Exxon Valdez Disaster.* Pullman: Washington State University Press, 2014, p. 4.

Page 9, line 3: Alaska Oil Spill Commission. S*pill: The Wreck of the Exxon Valdez: Implications for Safe Transportation of Oil.* February 1990. 26 Sept. 2017. http://www.arlis.org/docs/vol1/B/33339870.pdf

Page 12, line 11: *Red Light to Starboard: Recalling the Exxon Valdez Disaster,* p. 19.

Page 12, line 28: Sharon Bushell and Stan Jones, eds. *The Spill: Personal Stories from the Exxon Valdez Disaster.* Kenmore, Wash.: Epicenter Press, 2009, p. 40.

Page 16, line 6: Perry Collins. "Russian America: Letter from Mr. Collins to Secretary Seward." *The New York Times.* 9 April 1867, p. 1.

Page 25, line 23: *Not One Drop: Betrayal and Courage in the Wake of the Exxon Valdez Oil Spill,* p. 33.

Page 26, line 22: *The Spill: Personal Stories from the Exxon Valdez Disaster,* p. 63.

Page 28, line 25: *Red Light to Starboard: Recalling the Exxon Valdez Disaster,* p. 29.

Page 32, line 10: *The Spill: Personal Stories from the Exxon Valdez Disaster,* p. 158.

Page 33, line 9: Ibid., p. 161.

Page 35, line 5: Ibid., p. 107.

Page 37, line 9: Ibid., p. 145.

Page 38, line 2: Bob Hallinen. Email interview. 22 June 2017.

Page 38, line 12: Ibid.

Page 38, line 28: Ibid.

Page 41, col. 2, line 6: *The Spill: Personal Stories from the Exxon Valdez Disaster,* p. 282.

Page 42, line 12: *Not One Drop: Betrayal and Courage in the Wake of the Exxon Valdez Oil Spill,* p. 73.

Page 42, line 22: Ibid., p. 55.

Page 44, line 17: National Response Team. "The Exxon Valdez Oil Spill: A Report to the President." U.S. Environmental Protection Agency. May 1989. 26 Sept. 2017. nepis.epa.gov/Exe/ZyPURL.cgi?Dockey=10003M19.TXT

Page 44, line 26: *Spill: The Wreck of the Exxon Valdez: Implications for Safe Transportation of Oil,* p. 206.

Page 47, col. 2, line 10: Allan Turner. "Tanker's double hull prevented major spill off Galveston." *Houston Chronicle.* 11 March 2009. 26 Sept. 2017. http://www.chron.com/news/houston-texas/article/Tanker-s-double-hull-prevented-major-spill-off-1731407.php

Page 49, line 23: Keith Schneider. "Jury Finds Exxon Acted Recklessly in Valdez Oil Spill." *The New York Times.* 14 June 1994. 26 Sept. 2017. http://www.nytimes.com/1994/06/14/us/jury-finds-exxon-acted-recklessly-in-valdez-oil-spill.html

Page 50, line 3: Ibid.

Page 52, line 1: *The Spill: Personal Stories from the Exxon Valdez Disaster,* p. 212.

Page 53, line 12: Elizabeth Shogren. "Why the Exxon Valdez Spill Was a Eureka Moment for Science." *All Things Considered.* NPR. 22 March 2014. 26 Sept. 2017. http://www.npr.org/2014/03/22/292131305/why-the-exxon-valdez-spill-was-a-eureka-moment-for-science

Page 54, line 8: "The Valdez Oil Spill." ExxonMobil. 26 Sept. 2017. http://corporate.exxonmobil.com/en/environment/emergency-preparedness/spill-prevention-and-response/valdez-oil-spill

Page 54, line 22: Bob Hallinen. Email interview. 22 June 2017.

Page 54, line 28: Ibid.

Select Bibliography

Alaska History and Cultural Studies. 26 Sept. 2017. http://www.akhistorycourse.org/russias-colony/table-of-contents

Alaska Oil Spill Commission. *Spill: The Wreck of the Exxon Valdez: Implications for Safe Transportation of Oil.* February 1990. 26 Sept. 2017. http://www.arlis.org/docs/vol1/B/33339870.pdf

Alaska Permanent Fund Corporation. 26 Sept. 2017. http://www.apfc.org/home/Content/home/index.cfm

Alyeska Pipeline Service Company. 26 Sept. 2017. http://www.alyeska-pipe.com/

Associated Press. "Mate on Exxon Valdez Tells About Tanker's Striking Reef." *The New York Times.* 14 Feb. 1990. 26 Sept. 2017. http://www.nytimes.com/1990/02/14/us/mate-on-exxon-valdez-tells-about-tanker-s-striking-reef.html

Berliner, Jeff. "Record Alaska salmon catch despite spill." United Press International. 26 Sept. 1989. 26 Sept. 2017. http://www.upi.com/Archives/1989/09/26/Record-Alaska-salmon-catch-despite-spill/1968622785600/

Bushell, Sharon, and Stan Jones, eds. *The Spill: Personal Stories from the Exxon Valdez Disaster.* Kenmore, Wash.: Epicenter Press, 2009.

Collins, Perry. "Russian America: Letter from Mr. Collins to Secretary Seward." *The New York Times.* 9 April 1867, p. 1.

Day, Angela. *Red Light to Starboard: Recalling the Exxon Valdez Disaster.* Pullman: Washington State University Press, 2014.

Egan, Timothy. "Alaskan Oil Spill Laid to Collapse of Regulation." *The New York Times.* 6 Jan. 1990. 26 Sept. 2017. http://www.nytimes.com/1990/01/06/us/alaskan-oil-spill-laid-to-collapse-of-regulation.html

Epler, Patti Epler. "The events after the grounding." *Alaska Dispatch News.* 14 May 1989. Updated 1 July 2016. 26 Sept. 2017. https://www.adn.com/exxon-valdez-oil-spill/article/countdown-disaster/1989/05/14/

"Exxon Valdez Oil Spill." Office of Response and Restoration. National Oceanic and Atmospheric Administration. 26 Sept. 2017. http://response.restoration.noaa.gov/oil-and-chemical-spills/significant-incidents/exxon-valdez-oil-spill

Exxon Valdez Oil Spill Trustee Council. "Details About the Accident." Alaska Resources Library & Information Services. 26 Sept. 2017. http://www.evostc.state.ak.us/index.cfm?FA=facts.details

"A Final Farewell to Oil Tankers with Single Hulls." Office of Response and Restoration. National Oceanic and Atmospheric Administration. 11 Dec. 2014. 26 Sept. 2017. http://response.restoration.noaa.gov/about/media/final-farewell-oil-tankers-single-hulls.html

"The Fur Rush: The Russian-American Company." LitSite Alaska. The University of Alaska Anchorage. 26 Sept. 2017. http://www.litsite.org/index.cfm%3Fsection%3DTimeline%26page%3DRussian-America%26cat%3DAlaska's-Fur-Rush:-The-Russian-America-Company%26viewpost%3D2%26ContentId%3D2845

Grandoni, Dino, Asaf Shalev, Michael Phillis, and Susanne Rust. "The role a melting glacier played in Exxon's biggest disaster." *Los Angeles Times.* 6 April 2017. 26 Sept. 2017. http://www.latimes.com/projects/la-na-exxon-valdez/

"The Great M9.2 Alaska Earthquake and Tsunami of March 27, 1964." U.S. Geological Survey. 26 Sept. 2017. https://earthquake.usgs.gov/earthquakes/events/alaska1964/

Hayes, Thomas C. "Profits Off at Chevron and Exxon." *The New York Times.* 25 Jan. 1990. 26 Sept. 2017. http://www.nytimes.com/1990/01/25/business/company-earnings-profits-off-at-chevron-and-exxon.html?pagewanted=all

Holba, Carrie, and Helen Woods. "Exxon Valdez Oil Spill: FAQs, Links, and Unique Resources." Alaska Resources Library & Information Services. Updated 30 June 2017. 26 Sept. 2017. www.arlis.org/docs/vol2/a/EVOS_FAQs.pdf

"Judge Accepts Exxon Pact, Ending Suits on Valdez Spill." *The New York Times.* 9 Oct. 1991. 26 Sept. 2017. http://www.nytimes.com/1991/10/09/us/judge-accepts-exxon-pact-ending-suits-on-valdez-spill.html

Letter from Fred A. Seaton, secretary of the Interior, to President Dwight D. Eisenhower Regarding Alaska's Readiness for Statehood. 24 June 1958. 26 Sept. 2017. Eisenhower Presidential Library. https://www.eisenhower.archives.gov/research/online_documents/alaska_statehood/1958_06_24_Seaton_to_DDE.pdf

Mauer, Richard. "Alaska Aide Assails Oil Industry For 'Inadequate' Response to Spill." *The New York Times.* 26 March 1989. 26 Sept. 2017. http://www.nytimes.com/1989/03/26/us/alaska-aide-assails-oil-industry-for-inadequate-response-to-spill.html

Murkowski, Lisa. "Senator Murkowski addressing the Supreme Court Hearing of Exxon Valdez Oil Spill Case." 26 Feb. 2008. 26 Sept. 2017. https://www.murkowski.senate.gov/press/speech/senator-murkowski-addressing-the-supreme-court-hearing-of-exxon-valdez-oil-spill-case

National Response Team. "The Exxon Valdez Oil Spill: A Report to the President." U.S. Environmental Protection Agency. May 1989. 26 Sept. 2017. nepis.epa.gov/Exe/ZyPURL.cgi?Dockey=10003M19.TXT

Oil Spill Recovery Institute. 26 Sept. 2017. http://www.pws-osri.org/

Ott, Riki. *Not One Drop: Betrayal and Courage in the Wake of the Exxon Valdez Oil Spill.* White River Junction, Vt.: Chelsea Green Publishing, 2008.

Pletcher, David M. *The Diplomacy of Involvement: American Economic Expansion Across the Pacific, 1784-1900.* Columbia: University of Missouri Press, 2001.

Restino, Carey. "Recalling the shock and sadness of Exxon Valdez spill 25 years ago." *Alaska Dispatch News.* 22 March 2014. Updated 28 Sept. 2016. 26 Sept. 2017. https://www.adn.com/alaska-news/article/recalling-shock-and-sadness-exxon-valdez-spill-25-years-ago/2014/03/23/

Saulitis, Eva. *Into Great Silence: A Memoir of Discovery and Loss among Vanishing Orcas.* Boston: Beacon Press, 2012.

Schneider, Keith. "Jury Finds Exxon Acted Recklessly in Valdez Oil Spill." *The New York Times.* 14 June 1994. 26 Sept. 2017. http://www.nytimes.com/1994/06/14/us/jury-finds-exxon-acted-recklessly-in-valdez-oil-spill.html

Sheppard, Kate. "25 Years After Exxon Valdez Spill, Environmental Advocates Say Oil Laws Outdated." *HuffPost.* 24 March 2014. 26 Sept. 2017. http://www.huffingtonpost.com/2014/03/24/exxon-valdez-oil-spill_n_5022839.html

"Ship Captain Acquitted of Felony But Is Convicted on Minor Charge." *The New York Times.* 23 March 1990. 26 Sept. 2017. http://www.nytimes.com/1990/03/23/us/ship-captain-acquitted-of-felony-but-is-convicted-on-minor-charge.html?pagewanted=all

Shogren, Elizabeth. "Why the Exxon Valdez Spill Was a Eureka Moment for Science." *All Things Considered.* NPR. 22 March 2014. 26 Sept. 2017. http://www.npr.org/2014/03/22/292131305/why-the-exxon-valdez-spill-was-a-eureka-moment-for-science

Stranahan, Susan Q. "The Valdez Crud." *Mother Jones.* March/April 2003. 26 Sept. 2017. http://www.motherjones.com/politics/2003/03/valdez-crud/

Summary of the Oil Pollution Act. U.S. Environmental Protection Agency. 26 Sept. 2017. https://www.epa.gov/laws-regulations/summary-oil-pollution-act

Witkin, Richard, Andrew H. Malcolm, and Roberto Suro. "How the Oil Spilled and Spread: Delay and Confusion Off Alaska." *The New York Times.* 16 April 1989. 26 Sept. 2017. http://www.nytimes.com/1989/04/16/us/how-the-oil-spilled-and-spread-delay-and-confusion-off-alaska.html

Index

About the Author

Michael Burgan has written many books for children and young adults during his 20 years as a freelance writer. Most of his books have focused on history. Burgan has won several awards for his writing. He lives in Santa Fe, New Mexico.